Lowriders

BY JACK DAVID

TEXAS
C ME DIP
CLASSIC AUTO

BELLWETHER MEDIA • MINNEAPOLIS, MN

Are you ready to take it to the extreme?
Torque books thrust you into the action-packed world
of sports, vehicles, and adventure. These books may
include dirt, smoke, fire, and dangerous stunts.

WARNING: READ AT YOUR OWN RISK.

This edition first published in 2008 by Bellwether Media.

No part of this publication may be reproduced in whole or in part without written permission of the publisher. For information regarding permission, write to Bellwether Media Inc., Attention: Permissions Department, Post Office Box 19349, Minneapolis, MN 55419.

Library of Congress Cataloging-in-Publication Data

David, Jack, 1968-
  Lowriders / by Jack David.
      p. cm. -- (Torque--cool rides)
  Summary: "Full color photography accompanies engaging information about Lowriders. The combination of high-interest subject matter and light text is intended for students in grades 3 through 7"--Provided by publisher.
  Includes bibliographical references and index.
  ISBN-13: 978-1-60014-150-8 (hardcover : alk. paper)
  ISBN-10: 1-60014-150-1 (hardcover : alk. paper)
  1. Lowriders--Juvenile literature. 2. Automobiles--Customizing--Juvenile literature.
I. Title.

  TL255.2.D38 2008
  629.222--dc22

                                                            2007040564

Contents

What Is a Lowrider?

The Canadian Kid

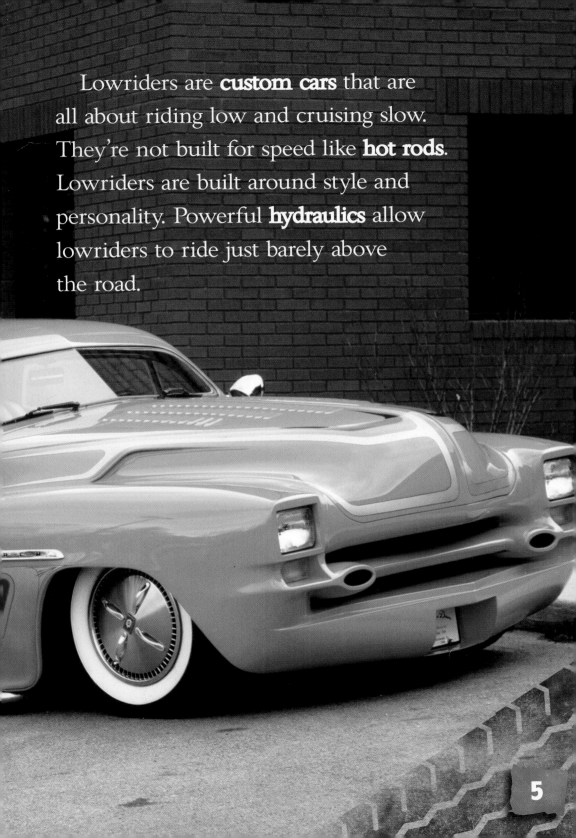

Lowriders are **custom cars** that are all about riding low and cruising slow. They're not built for speed like **hot rods**. Lowriders are built around style and personality. Powerful **hydraulics** allow lowriders to ride just barely above the road.

Fancy paint jobs, **chrome** parts, and thumping sound systems help complete the style. Every lowrider is unique. They're more than just cars. They're rolling works of art.

Lowrider History

Lowriding began in California in the late 1930s. Young Mexican Americans were buying their first cars. Some didn't have extra money for new parts or powerful engines. They bought inexpensive cars and fixed them up. They liked cars that rode low to the ground. They added heavy bags of sand to the trunks to make the cars ride low.

Lowriders have changed a lot since then. Hydraulics have replaced sandbags. The craze is no longer just among Mexican Americans. These days lowriders are popular with all kinds of people. Lowriding is even popular in Japan and Europe.

Fast Fact

A man named Ron Aguirre built the first hydraulic system for a lowrider. He used spare parts that he got from an old airplane.

Lowrider Features

The hydraulic system is a lowrider's most important feature. Pumps force fluid into and out of **cylinders** above each wheel. The fluid raises and lowers the body of the car. An owner can set the hydraulics so that the car's body barely clears the road.

TEXAS LOWRIDER CLUB

Fast FaCt

There are many classes of lowriders. A bomb is a lowrider built from a car from 1958 or earlier. A traditional is a car built from 1959 to the mid-1970s. A radical is a high-priced, new lowrider.

Other lowrider features are just for looks. Many owners coat the car's metal parts in a shiny layer of chrome. Some even chrome-plate the entire engine! Custom paint jobs are also common. Many owners paint **murals** on their cars. These paintings show loved ones, historical figures, religious symbols, and many other things.

Owners also customize the inside of the car. They may add soft velvet fabric and carpet. Big bucket seats provide extra comfort. Huge speakers and CD players can give the sound system a big boost. You can often hear a lowrider coming down the road long before you see it!

LOWriders in ActiOn

Lowrider owners love to show off their cars. They join clubs, drive in parades, or they cruise down the street.

Custom car shows are a great place to see lowriders. Judges award prizes to the best, most original designs. Some shows even have contests to show off hydraulics. In a hopping contest, owners use hydraulics to make a lowrider's front end jump off the ground. The car that jumps the highest is the winner. In a dancing contest, the car that best keeps to the beat of music is the winner. These are just a few of the ways that lowrider owners show off their unique cars.

Fast Fact

Hydraulic systems need lots of power. Many lowriders have huge banks of batteries in the trunk.

Glossary

chrome–a metallic substance called chromium; chrome gives metal objects a shiny look.

custom car–a car changed to suit an owner's tastes

cylinder–a tube into which hydraulic fluid is pumped; hydraulic cylinders are different from engine cylinders.

hot rod–a custom car built for speed

hydraulics–a system of pumps that force fluid into cylinders in order to lift a heavy object, such as a lowrider

mural–a large painting on the body of a lowrider

To Learn More

AT THE LIBRARY

Doeden, Matt. *Lowriders*. Mankato, Minn.: Capstone, 2005.

Maurer, Tracy Nelson. *Lowriders.* Vero Beach, Fla.: Rourke, 2004.

Poolos, Jamie. *Wild About Lowriders*. New York: Powerkids, 2008.

ON THE WEB

Learning more about lowriders is as easy as 1, 2, 3.

1. Go to www.factsurfer.com

2. Enter "lowriders" into search box.

3. Click the "Surf" button and you will see a list of related web sites.

With factsurfer.com, finding more information is just a click away.

23

Index

Bellwether wishes to thank John Torres and the Firme Lowrider Club of Houston.

The images in this book are reproduced through the courtesy of: John Torres/Nite Scenes, front cover, pp. 14, 15, 17, 21; National Motor Museum/Alamy, pp. 4-5; Joseph Sohm/Visions of America, LLC/Alamy, pp. 8-9; Ted Soqui/Corbis, pp.7, 16, 18-19; Sonja Pacho/zefa/Corbis, p. 10; Juan Martinez, p. 11; Suzanne Tucker, pp. 12-13.